Hello Winter!

Shelley Rotner

Holiday House New York

The trees are almost bare.

The days are getting

shorter and colder.

Winter is on its way.

Soon, it's the shortest day of the year
and the first day of winter—the winter solstice.

The sun sets early.

People make **fires** and sing songs.

There's a **chill** in the air.

Trees and plants stop growing
and wait for warm spring days.

Shadows are long.

It's cold!

Ponds and rivers start to freeze.

Ice crystals make delicate designs.

We can't wait for snow!

And then **snowflakes** start to fall and fall.

Hurray! It's a **snow day**!

We bundle up—mittens and hats,

jackets and boots.

We make snowballs,

snow **forts,**

and snow **people.**

We sled and slide.

We ski and skate.

We snowshoe

and **snowboard.**

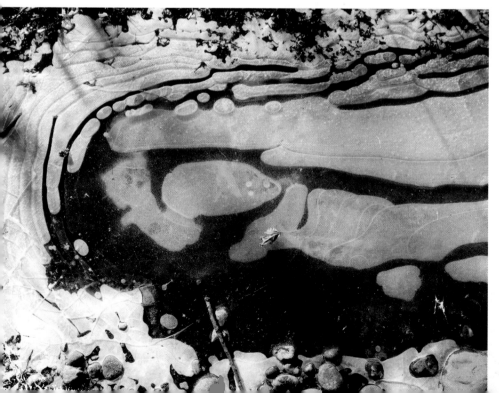

Frozen icicles hang.

Beautiful ice patterns form.

Hot chocolate
and a fire keep us warm.

Animals must keep warm too.

They adapt to the cold weather.

Birds grow more feathers.

They leave **tracks** in freshly fallen snow.

Some animals build nests or find shelter.

Others slow down.

Some go underground or underwater to keep warm.

Other animals sleep, or hibernate, for the whole winter.

In winter's **short** days,
we **celebrate** holidays
with **lights** and decorations.

Then the sun grows stronger.

Snow and ice melt.

The ground thaws and warms.

Trees and plants begin to wake up.

The days get longer and longer.

And then spring is finally here!

Glossary

Adapt—when animals or plants change to make living in a particular environment easier (for example, when a mammal grows more hair to stay warmer in the winter)

Hibernate—when animals spend the winter in an inactive state

Ice crystals—the formation of ice patterns in different shapes

Icicle—a hanging piece of ice that forms when dripping water freezes

Mammal—a warm-blooded animal with a backbone and skin mostly covered with hair that produces milk to feed its young

Spring equinox—the day in late March on which day and night last just about the same number of hours

Thaw—when warm weather following a freeze causes snow and ice to melt

Tracks—the impressions of animal footprints left in snow, soil, sand, or mud

Winter solstice—the shortest day of the year with the least amount of sunlight

Dedicated to my mom.

Special thanks to designer Katie Craig.

Copyright © 2018 by Shelley Rotner
All Rights Reserved
HOLIDAY HOUSE is registered in
the U.S. Patent and Trademark Office.
Printed and Bound in June 2018 at Tien
Wah Press, Johor Bahru, Johor, Malaysia.
www.holidayhouse.com
First Edition
1 3 5 7 9 10 8 6 4 2

Library of Congress Cataloging-in-
Publication Data is available.

ISBN 978-0-8234-3976-8 (hardcover)